Stuff
I Can't
Remember

A Personal
Organizer
for Passwords,
Birthdays, and
Other Crap You
Always Forget

CAITLIN PETERSON

CASTLE POINT BOOKS

NEW YORK

Contents

Get It Write!

I've learned two important lessons in life. I can't recall the first one, but the second one is that I need to start writing stuff down.

Sound familiar? That's exactly the idea behind *Stuff I Can't Remember*! It's a place to collect a crap-ton of details for modern daily life so you can spend more time and energy actually living it.

There's no shame in freeing your mind of strings of letters, numbers, and special characters. Access online accounts quickly and easily, so you can get what you need and move on with your glorious day. There's no reason you need to have your niece's birthday imprinted in your memory. Leave space for more creative endeavors, like choosing the perfect card or gift to send! Focus on special moments with family and friends, not swearing as you search for a crumpled sticky note with the information you need.

From your health history at a glance to the name of that plumber your neighbor recommended, one simple logbook has it all covered. Set it in print, then don't ever forget it!

Special Days to Celebrate

Never miss another birthday or anniversary!
Special days are meant to be shared with loved ones and
celebrated with a side of cake, not stress you out. Fill in
your special dates month by month, day by day to create
a perpetual calendar that will be your lifesaver.

TIPS

* Use the gift planning pages (30–32) to save all your
  brilliant ideas as inspiration hits.
* Set a date toward the end of each month (say, the
  25th) to look ahead and purchase cards and gifts
  for the upcoming month. One day, all done!

January

1

2

3

4

5

6

7

8

9

10

11

12

13

14

15

16

17
....

....

18
....

....

19
....

....

20
....

....

21
....

....

22
....

....

23
....

....

24
....

....

25
....

....

26
....

....

27
....

....

28
....

....

29
....

....

30
....

....

31
....

....

February

1

2

3

4

5

6

7

8

9

10

11

12

13

14

15

16

17

18

19

20

21

22

23

24

25

26

27

28

29

You can always trust me.
Not to remember anything without
writing it down. Not alone with cake.
But other than that.

March

1

2

3

4

5

6

7

8

9

10

11

12

13

14

15

16

17

....

....

18

....

....

19

....

....

20

....

....

21

....

....

22

....

....

23

....

....

24

....

....

25

....

....

26

....

....

27

....

....

28

....

....

29

....

....

30

....

....

31

....

....

April

1

2

3

4

5

6

7

8

9

10

11

12

13

14

15

16

17

18

19

20

21

22

23

24

25

26

27

28

29

30

Birthdays are good for your health. Studies show people who have them live longer.

May

1

2

3

4

5

6

7

8

9

10

11

12

13

14

15

16

17

....

....

18

....

....

19

....

....

20

....

....

21

....

....

22

....

....

23

....

....

24

....

....

25

....

....

26

....

....

27

....

....

28

....

....

29

....

....

30

....

....

31

....

....

June

1

2

3

4

5

6

7

8

9

10

11

12

13

14

15

16

17
....

....

18
....

....

19
....

....

20
....

....

21
....

....

22
....

....

23
....

....

24
....

....

25
....

....

26
....

....

27
....

....

28
....

....

29
....

....

30
....

....

The important thing to remember
is that I'm probably going to forget.

July

1

2

3

4

5

6

7

8

9

10

11

12

13

14

15

16

17

....

....

18

....

....

19

....

....

20

....

....

21

....

....

22

....

....

23

....

....

24

....

....

25

....

....

26

....

....

27

....

....

28

....

....

29

....

....

30

....

....

31

....

....

August

1

2

3

4

5

6

7

8

9

10

11

12

13

14

15

16

17
....

18
....

19
....

20
....

21
....

22
....

23
....

24
....
....

25
....

26
....

27
....

28
....

29
....

30
....

31
....
....

September

1

2

3

4

5

6

7

8

9

10

11

12

13

14

15

16

17
....

18
....

19
....

20
....

21
....

22
....

23
....

24
....

25
....

26
....

27
....

28
....

29
....

30
....

Eat cake. It's somebody's birthday somewhere.

October

1

2

3

4

5

6

7

8

9

10

11

12

13

14

15

16

17 ....

18 ....

19 ....

20 ....

21 ....

22 ....

23 ....

24 ....

25 ....

26 ....

27 ....

28 ....

29 ....

30 ....

31 ....

November

1

2

3

4

5

6

7

8

9

10

11

12

13

14

15

16

17

24

18

25

19

26

20

27

21

28

22

29

23

30

**If my memory gets any worse,
I'll be able to plan
my own surprise party.**

December

1
....

....

2
....

....

3
....

....

4
....

....

5
....

....

6
....

....

7
....

....

8
....

....

9
....

....

10
....

....

11
....

....

12
....

....

13
....

....

14
....

....

15
....

....

16
....

....

17
....

18
....

19
....

20
....

21
....

22
....

23
....

24
....

25
....

26
....

27
....

28
....

29
....

30
....

31
....

GREAT GIFT IDEAS

Gift	Cost	Occasion	Recipient

GREAT GIFT IDEAS

Gift	Cost	Occasion	Recipient

GREAT GIFT IDEAS

Gift	Cost	Occasion	Recipient

Password Peace of Mind

No more password prompt nightmares or getting lost in a resetting cycle! Burn all those sticky notes and still feel confident you have immediate access to all your online accounts, even as you make your passwords unique and trickier (and more secure!).

TIPS

* "Password" and "123456" basically spell out "break into my account." Also avoid using a birthday, anniversary, address, city of birth, high school, or family (even pet) name.
* Mix up symbols and numbers with letters. Capitalize some random letters too.
* Think up a sentence and use only the first two letters of each word. Aim for 14 characters long. ("Too old to remember all this crap" becomes "ToOltoReAlthCR.")

Internet service provider

Account number

Technical support

Customer service

Wi-Fi location

Wi-Fi network

Password   **Date set**

Password   **Date set**

Wi-Fi location

Wi-Fi network

Password   **Date set**

Password   **Date set**

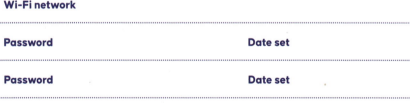

"Be strong," I whispered to my Wi-Fi signal.

Internet service provider
....

Account number
....

Technical support
....

Customer service
....

Wi-Fi location
....

Wi-Fi network
....

Password   **Date set**
....

Password   **Date set**
....

Wi-Fi location
....

Wi-Fi network
....

Password   **Date set**
....

Password   **Date set**
....

Memory loss is like underwear.
It creeps up on you.

Email

....

Password   **Date set**

....

Password   **Date set**

....

Email

....

Password   **Date set**

....

Password   **Date set**

....

Email

....

Password   **Date set**

....

Password   **Date set**

....

Email

....

Password   **Date set**

....

Password   **Date set**

....

Website

Login / username

Password   **Date set**

Password   **Date set**

Notes

Website

Login / username

Password   **Date set**

Password   **Date set**

Notes

Website

Login / username

Password   **Date set**

Password   **Date set**

Notes

A

Website

....

Login / username

....

Password   **Date set**

....

Password   **Date set**

....

Notes

....

Website

....

Login / username

....

Password   **Date set**

....

Password   **Date set**

....

Notes

....

Website

....

Login / username

....

Password   **Date set**

....

Password   **Date set**

....

Notes

....

Website

....

Login / username

....

Password   **Date set**

....

Password   **Date set**

....

Notes

....

Website

....

Login / username

....

Password   **Date set**

....

Password   **Date set**

....

Notes

....

Website

....

Login / username

....

Password   **Date set**

....

Password   **Date set**

....

Notes

....

B

Website

Login / username

Password   **Date set**

Password   **Date set**

Notes

Website

Login / username

Password   **Date set**

Password   **Date set**

Notes

Website

Login / username

Password   **Date set**

Password   **Date set**

Notes

Website

....

Login / username

....

Password   **Date set**

....

Password   **Date set**

....

Notes

....

Website

....

Login / username

....

Password   **Date set**

....

Password   **Date set**

....

Notes

....

Website

....

Login / username

....

Password   **Date set**

....

Password   **Date set**

....

Notes

....

B

Website
....

Login / username
....

Password   **Date set**
....

Password   **Date set**
....

Notes
....

Website
....

Login / username
....

Password   **Date set**
....

Password   **Date set**
....

Notes
....

Website
....

Login / username
....

Password   **Date set**
....

Password   **Date set**
....

Notes
....

Website

....

Login / username

....

Password   **Date set**

....

Password   **Date set**

....

Notes

....

Website

....

Login / username

....

Password   **Date set**

....

Password   **Date set**

....

Notes

....

Website

....

Login / username

....

Password   **Date set**

....

Password   **Date set**

....

Notes

....

Website

Login / username

Password   **Date set**

Password   **Date set**

Notes

Website

Login / username

Password   **Date set**

Password   **Date set**

Notes

Website

Login / username

Password   **Date set**

Password   **Date set**

Notes

Website

Login / username

Password   **Date set**

Password   **Date set**

Notes

Website

Login / username

Password   **Date set**

Password   **Date set**

Notes

My ability to remember crappy song lyrics far exceeds my ability to remember passwords.

D

Website

....

Login / username

....

Password   **Date set**

....

Password   **Date set**

....

Notes

....

Website

....

Login / username

....

Password   **Date set**

....

Password   **Date set**

....

Notes

....

Website

....

Login / username

....

Password   **Date set**

....

Password   **Date set**

....

Notes

....

Website

Login / username

Password   **Date set**

Password   **Date set**

Notes

Website

Login / username

Password   **Date set**

Password   **Date set**

Notes

Website

Login / username

Password   **Date set**

Password   **Date set**

Notes

Website

Login / username

Password   **Date set**

Password   **Date set**

Notes

Website

Login / username

Password   **Date set**

Password   **Date set**

Notes

Website

Login / username

Password   **Date set**

Password   **Date set**

Notes

Website

....

Login / username

....

Password   **Date set**

....

Password   **Date set**

....

Notes

....

Website

....

Login / username

....

Password   **Date set**

....

Password   **Date set**

....

Notes

....

Website

....

Login / username

....

Password   **Date set**

....

Password   **Date set**

....

Notes

....

Website

Login / username

Password   **Date set**

Password   **Date set**

Notes

Website

Login / username

Password   **Date set**

Password   **Date set**

Notes

Website

Login / username

Password   **Date set**

Password   **Date set**

Notes

Website

Login / username

Password   **Date set**

Password   **Date set**

Notes

Website

Login / username

Password   **Date set**

Password   **Date set**

Notes

Website

Login / username

Password   **Date set**

Password   **Date set**

Notes

Website

Login / username

Password   **Date set**

Password   **Date set**

Notes

Website

Login / username

Password   **Date set**

Password   **Date set**

Notes

Website

Login / username

Password   **Date set**

Password   **Date set**

Notes

F

Website
....

Login / username
....

Password   **Date set**
....

Password   **Date set**
....

Notes
....

Website
....

Login / username
....

Password   **Date set**
....

Password   **Date set**
....

Notes
....

Website
....

Login / username
....

Password   **Date set**
....

Password   **Date set**
....

Notes
....

F

Website
....

Login / username
....

Password   **Date set**
....

Password   **Date set**
....

Notes
....

Website
....

Login / username
....

Password   **Date set**
....

Password   **Date set**
....

Notes
....

Website
....

Login / username
....

Password   **Date set**
....

Password   **Date set**
....

Notes
....

Website

....

Login / username

....

Password   **Date set**

....

Password   **Date set**

....

Notes

....

Website

....

Login / username

....

Password   **Date set**

....

Password   **Date set**

....

Notes

....

Website

....

Login / username

....

Password   **Date set**

....

Password   **Date set**

....

Notes

....

G

Website

....

Login / username

....

Password   **Date set**

....

Password   **Date set**

....

Notes

....

Website

....

Login / username

....

Password   **Date set**

....

Password   **Date set**

....

Notes

....

The most important thing to remember: Home is where you take your pants off.

Website

Login / username

Password   **Date set**

Password   **Date set**

Notes

Website

Login / username

Password   **Date set**

Password   **Date set**

Notes

Website

Login / username

Password   **Date set**

Password   **Date set**

Notes

Website

....

Login / username

....

Password   **Date set**

....

Password   **Date set**

....

Notes

....

Website

....

Login / username

....

Password   **Date set**

....

Password   **Date set**

....

Notes

....

Website

....

Login / username

....

Password   **Date set**

....

Password   **Date set**

....

Notes

....

Website

Login / username

Password   **Date set**

Password   **Date set**

Notes

Website

Login / username

Password   **Date set**

Password   **Date set**

Notes

Website

Login / username

Password   **Date set**

Password   **Date set**

Notes

Website

....

Login / username

....

Password   **Date set**

....

Password   **Date set**

....

Notes

....

Website

....

Login / username

....

Password   **Date set**

....

Password   **Date set**

....

Notes

....

Website

....

Login / username

....

Password   **Date set**

....

Password   **Date set**

....

Notes

....

Website

....

Login / username

....

Password   **Date set**

....

Password   **Date set**

....

Notes

....

Website

....

Login / username

....

Password   **Date set**

....

Password   **Date set**

....

Notes

....

Website

....

Login / username

....

Password   **Date set**

....

Password   **Date set**

....

Notes

....

Website

Login / username

Password   **Date set**

Password   **Date set**

Notes

Website

Login / username

Password   **Date set**

Password   **Date set**

Notes

Website

Login / username

Password   **Date set**

Password   **Date set**

Notes

I

Website

Login / username

Password   **Date set**

Password   **Date set**

Notes

Website

Login / username

Password   **Date set**

Password   **Date set**

Notes

Website

Login / username

Password   **Date set**

Password   **Date set**

Notes

Website

Login / username

Password   **Date set**

Password   **Date set**

Notes

Website

Login / username

Password   **Date set**

Password   **Date set**

Notes

Website

Login / username

Password   **Date set**

Password   **Date set**

Notes

Website

Login / username

Password   **Date set**

Password   **Date set**

Notes

Website

Login / username

Password   **Date set**

Password   **Date set**

Notes

Website: We use cookies to improve performance. Me: Same!

Website

....

Login / username

....

Password   **Date set**

....

Password   **Date set**

....

Notes

....

Website

....

Login / username

....

Password   **Date set**

....

Password   **Date set**

....

Notes

....

Website

....

Login / username

....

Password   **Date set**

....

Password   **Date set**

....

Notes

....

Website

Login / username

Password   **Date set**

Password   **Date set**

Notes

Website

Login / username

Password   **Date set**

Password   **Date set**

Notes

Website

Login / username

Password   **Date set**

Password   **Date set**

Notes

Website

Login / username

Password **Date set**

Password **Date set**

Notes

Website

Login / username

Password **Date set**

Password **Date set**

Notes

Website

Login / username

Password **Date set**

Password **Date set**

Notes

Website
....

Login / username
....

Password   **Date set**
....

Password   **Date set**
....

Notes
....

Website
....

Login / username
....

Password   **Date set**
....

Password   **Date set**
....

Notes
....

Website
....

Login / username
....

Password   **Date set**
....

Password   **Date set**
....

Notes
....

Website

Login / username

Password   **Date set**

Password   **Date set**

Notes

Website

Login / username

Password   **Date set**

Password   **Date set**

Notes

Website

Login / username

Password   **Date set**

Password   **Date set**

Notes

Website

Login / username

Password   **Date set**

Password   **Date set**

Notes

Website

Login / username

Password   **Date set**

Password   **Date set**

Notes

Website

Login / username

Password   **Date set**

Password   **Date set**

Notes

Website

....

Login / username

....

Password   **Date set**

....

Password   **Date set**

....

Notes

....

Website

....

Login / username

....

Password   **Date set**

....

Password   **Date set**

....

Notes

....

Website

....

Login / username

....

Password   **Date set**

....

Password   **Date set**

....

Notes

....

Website

Login / username

Password   **Date set**

Password   **Date set**

Notes

Website

Login / username

Password   **Date set**

Password   **Date set**

Notes

Website

Login / username

Password   **Date set**

Password   **Date set**

Notes

Website

···

Login / username

···

Password   **Date set**

···

Password   **Date set**

···

Notes

···

Website

···

Login / username

···

Password   **Date set**

···

Password   **Date set**

···

Notes

···

Website

···

Login / username

···

Password   **Date set**

···

Password   **Date set**

···

Notes

···

Website

Login / username

Password   **Date set**

Password   **Date set**

Notes

Website

Login / username

Password   **Date set**

Password   **Date set**

Notes

Website

Login / username

Password   **Date set**

Password   **Date set**

Notes

Website

Login / username

Password   **Date set**

Password   **Date set**

Notes

Website

Login / username

Password   **Date set**

Password   **Date set**

Notes

Website

Login / username

Password   **Date set**

Password   **Date set**

Notes

Website
....

Login / username
....

Password   **Date set**
....

Password   **Date set**
....

Notes
....

Website
....

Login / username
....

Password   **Date set**
....

Password   **Date set**
....

Notes
....

Website
....

Login / username
....

Password   **Date set**
....

Password   **Date set**
....

Notes
....

Website

Login / username

Password   **Date set**

Password   **Date set**

Notes

Website

Login / username

Password   **Date set**

Password   **Date set**

Notes

Website

Login / username

Password   **Date set**

Password   **Date set**

Notes

O

Website

Login / username

Password   **Date set**

Password   **Date set**

Notes

Website

Login / username

Password   **Date set**

Password   **Date set**

Notes

Website

Login / username

Password   **Date set**

Password   **Date set**

Notes

Website

Login / username

Password   **Date set**

Password   **Date set**

Notes

Website

Login / username

Password   **Date set**

Password   **Date set**

Notes

I am wonder woman: I wonder where I left my keys and what that darn password is!

Website

Login / username

Password	**Date set**

Password	**Date set**

Notes

Website

Login / username

Password	**Date set**

Password	**Date set**

Notes

Website

Login / username

Password	**Date set**

Password	**Date set**

Notes

Website

....

Login / username

....

Password   **Date set**

....

Password   **Date set**

....

Notes

....

Website

....

Login / username

....

Password   **Date set**

....

Password   **Date set**

....

Notes

....

Website

....

Login / username

....

Password   **Date set**

....

Password   **Date set**

....

Notes

....

Website

Login / username

Password   **Date set**

Password   **Date set**

Notes

Website

Login / username

Password   **Date set**

Password   **Date set**

Notes

Website

Login / username

Password   **Date set**

Password   **Date set**

Notes

Website

....

Login / username

....

Password   **Date set**

....

Password   **Date set**

....

Notes

....

Website

....

Login / username

....

Password   **Date set**

....

Password   **Date set**

....

Notes

....

Website

....

Login / username

....

Password   **Date set**

....

Password   **Date set**

....

Notes

....

Website

Login / username

Password   **Date set**

Password   **Date set**

Notes

Website

Login / username

Password   **Date set**

Password   **Date set**

Notes

Website

Login / username

Password   **Date set**

Password   **Date set**

Notes

Website

....

Login / username

....

Password   **Date set**

....

Password   **Date set**

....

Notes

....

Website

....

Login / username

....

Password   **Date set**

....

Password   **Date set**

....

Notes

....

Website

....

Login / username

....

Password   **Date set**

....

Password   **Date set**

....

Notes

....

Q

Website
....

Login / username
....

Password   **Date set**
....

Password   **Date set**
....

Notes
....

Website
....

Login / username
....

Password   **Date set**
....

Password   **Date set**
....

Notes
....

On a scale of one to granola bar, how much is your memory falling apart?

Website

Login / username

Password   **Date set**

Password   **Date set**

Notes

Website

Login / username

Password   **Date set**

Password   **Date set**

Notes

Website

Login / username

Password   **Date set**

Password   **Date set**

Notes

Website

....

Login / username

....

Password   **Date set**

....

Password   **Date set**

....

Notes

....

Website

....

Login / username

....

Password   **Date set**

....

Password   **Date set**

....

Notes

....

Website

....

Login / username

....

Password   **Date set**

....

Password   **Date set**

....

Notes

....

Website

Login / username

Password   **Date set**

Password   **Date set**

Notes

Website

Login / username

Password   **Date set**

Password   **Date set**

Notes

Website

Login / username

Password   **Date set**

Password   **Date set**

Notes

Website

Login / username

Password   **Date set**

Password   **Date set**

Notes

Website

Login / username

Password   **Date set**

Password   **Date set**

Notes

Website

Login / username

Password   **Date set**

Password   **Date set**

Notes

Website

....

Login / username

....

Password   **Date set**

....

Password   **Date set**

....

Notes

....

Website

....

Login / username

....

Password   **Date set**

....

Password   **Date set**

....

Notes

....

Website

....

Login / username

....

Password   **Date set**

....

Password   **Date set**

....

Notes

....

S

Website

Login / username

Password   **Date set**

Password   **Date set**

Notes

Website

Login / username

Password   **Date set**

Password   **Date set**

Notes

Website

Login / username

Password   **Date set**

Password   **Date set**

Notes

Website

Login / username

Password   **Date set**

Password   **Date set**

Notes

Website

Login / username

Password   **Date set**

Password   **Date set**

Notes

Website

Login / username

Password   **Date set**

Password   **Date set**

Notes

Website

Login / username

Password   **Date set**

Password   **Date set**

Notes

Website

Login / username

Password   **Date set**

Password   **Date set**

Notes

Website

Login / username

Password   **Date set**

Password   **Date set**

Notes

Website

....

Login / username

....

Password   **Date set**

....

Password   **Date set**

....

Notes

....

Website

....

Login / username

....

Password   **Date set**

....

Password   **Date set**

....

Notes

....

Where's the "unsubscribe" button
on forgetting things?

Website

Login / username

Password   **Date set**

Password   **Date set**

Notes

Website

Login / username

Password   **Date set**

Password   **Date set**

Notes

Website

Login / username

Password   **Date set**

Password   **Date set**

Notes

Website

Login / username

Password   **Date set**

Password   **Date set**

Notes

Website

Login / username

Password   **Date set**

Password   **Date set**

Notes

Website

Login / username

Password   **Date set**

Password   **Date set**

Notes

Website

Login / username

Password   **Date set**

Password   **Date set**

Notes

Website

Login / username

Password   **Date set**

Password   **Date set**

Notes

Website

Login / username

Password   **Date set**

Password   **Date set**

Notes

V

Website

Login / username

Password   **Date set**

Password   **Date set**

Notes

Website

Login / username

Password   **Date set**

Password   **Date set**

Notes

Website

Login / username

Password   **Date set**

Password   **Date set**

Notes

Website

Login / username

Password   **Date set**

Password   **Date set**

Notes

Website

Login / username

Password   **Date set**

Password   **Date set**

Notes

Website

Login / username

Password   **Date set**

Password   **Date set**

Notes

Website

Login / username

Password   **Date set**

Password   **Date set**

Notes

Website

Login / username

Password   **Date set**

Password   **Date set**

Notes

Website

Login / username

Password   **Date set**

Password   **Date set**

Notes

Website

Login / username

Password   **Date set**

Password   **Date set**

Notes

Website

Login / username

Password   **Date set**

Password   **Date set**

Notes

Website

Login / username

Password   **Date set**

Password   **Date set**

Notes

Website

Login / username

Password   Date set

Password   Date set

Notes

Website

Login / username

Password   Date set

Password   Date set

Notes

Website

Login / username

Password   Date set

Password   Date set

Notes

Website

Login / username

Password   **Date set**

Password   **Date set**

Notes

Website

Login / username

Password   **Date set**

Password   **Date set**

Notes

I learn something new every day— and forget five other things.

X

Website

Login / username

Password   **Date set**

Password   **Date set**

Notes

Website

Login / username

Password   **Date set**

Password   **Date set**

Notes

Website

Login / username

Password   **Date set**

Password   **Date set**

Notes

Website

Login / username

Password   **Date set**

Password   **Date set**

Notes

Website

Login / username

Password   **Date set**

Password   **Date set**

Notes

Website

Login / username

Password   **Date set**

Password   **Date set**

Notes

Y

Website

Login / username

Password

Date set

Password

Date set

Notes

Website

Login / username

Password

Date set

Password

Date set

Notes

Website

Login / username

Password

Date set

Password

Date set

Notes

Website

Login / username

Password **Date set**

Password **Date set**

Notes

Website

Login / username

Password **Date set**

Password **Date set**

Notes

Website

Login / username

Password **Date set**

Password **Date set**

Notes

Website

Login / username

Password   **Date set**

Password   **Date set**

Notes

Website

Login / username

Password   **Date set**

Password   **Date set**

Notes

Website

Login / username

Password   **Date set**

Password   **Date set**

Notes

Z

Website

Login / username

Password   **Date set**

Password   **Date set**

Notes

Website

Login / username

Password   **Date set**

Password   **Date set**

Notes

Website

Login / username

Password   **Date set**

Password   **Date set**

Notes

Z

Website

Login / username

Password   **Date set**

Password   **Date set**

Notes

Website

Login / username

Password   **Date set**

Password   **Date set**

Notes

My years of forgetting experience
just keep adding up.

Financial Freedom

With so many numbers related to finances screwing with your head, surely you can take the pressure off by dropping some basic account information here. Share the location of this logbook with a trusty financial backup to make it easy for someone to jump in and help in an emergency.

TIPS

* If you need to set answers to security questions, choose ones that can't be learned from your social media accounts. Quiz your financial backup to make sure they know the answers.
* Review financial account activity almost as often as social media to monitor for security.

ACCOUNT OVERVIEWS

Financial institution
....

Account type
....

Account number
....

Contact
....

Notes
....

Financial institution
....

Account type
....

Account number
....

Contact
....

Notes
....

Financial institution
....

Account type
....

Account number
....

Contact
....

Notes
....

ACCOUNT OVERVIEWS

Financial institution
....

Account type
....

Account number
....

Contact
....

Notes
....

Financial institution
....

Account type
....

Account number
....

Contact
....

Notes
....

My favorite childhood memory is not paying bills.

PAYMENTS COMING IN

	Description	Amount	Account	Frequency
1				
2				
3				
4				
5				
6				
7				
8				
9				
10				
11				
12				
13				
14				
15				
16				

PAYMENTS COMING IN

	Description	Amount	Account	Frequency
17				
18				
19				
20				
21				
22				
23				
24				
25				
26				
27				
28				
29				
30				
31				

PAYMENTS GOING OUT

	Description	Amount	Account	Frequency
1				
2				
3				
4				
5				
6				
7				
8				
9				
10				
11				
12				
13				
14				
15				
16				

PAYMENTS GOING OUT

	Description	Amount	Account	Frequency
17				
18				
19				
20				
21				
22				
23				
24				
25				
26				
27				
28				
29				
30				
31				

PERSONAL LOANS

Borrower	Amount	Payment due

I swear I have it all together.
I just forgot where I put it.

Handy Home Records

You want to give your home top-notch care so it stays at its best for you. A little organization can make it easier to keep up with maintenance. And when stuff inevitably hits the fan, turning to the pro contacts you've gathered, and notes about any experiences with them, can make any repairs feel like less of a panic.

TIPS

* Break home maintenance crap into seasons and remember to consider both indoors and outdoors. Mark your calendar to start planning at the beginning of each season or even before the season hits.
* Collect recommendations and check references for home professionals before you need them.

SPRING MAINTENANCE REMINDERS

Task	Who will perform	Target date(s)	Completed date

Secret: I have no idea what the hell I'm doing.

SUMMER MAINTENANCE REMINDERS

Task	Who will perform	Target date(s)	Completed date

FALL MAINTENANCE REMINDERS

Task	Who will perform	Target date(s)	Completed date

WINTER MAINTENANCE REMINDERS

Task	Who will perform	Target date(s)	Completed date

SERVICE AND REPAIR HISTORY

Service/repair

....

Performed by

....

Date   **Notes**

....

Date   **Notes**

....

Service/repair

....

Performed by

....

Date   **Notes**

....

Date   **Notes**

....

Service/repair

....

Performed by

....

Date   **Notes**

....

Date   **Notes**

....

SERVICE AND REPAIR HISTORY

Service/repair

Performed by

Date   **Notes**

Date   **Notes**

Service/repair

Performed by

Date   **Notes**

Date   **Notes**

Service/repair

Performed by

Date   **Notes**

Date   **Notes**

SERVICE AND REPAIR HISTORY

Service/repair

....

Performed by

....

Date   **Notes**

....

Date   **Notes**

....

Service/repair

....

Performed by

....

Date   **Notes**

....

Date   **Notes**

....

I'm never sure if I actually have free time or if I just keep forgetting stuff.

SERVICE AND REPAIR HISTORY

Service/repair

....

Performed by

....

Date   **Notes**

....

Date   **Notes**

....

Service/repair

....

Performed by

....

Date   **Notes**

....

Date   **Notes**

....

Service/repair

....

Performed by

....

Date   **Notes**

....

Date   **Notes**

....

PROS TO CALL

Name

Services provided

Contact

Recommended by   **References checked?**

Notes

Name

Services provided

Contact

Recommended by   **References checked?**

Notes

Name

Services provided

Contact

Recommended by   **References checked?**

Notes

PROS TO CALL

Name
....

Services provided
....

Contact
....

Recommended by   **References checked?**
....

Notes
....

Name
....

Services provided
....

Contact
....

Recommended by   **References checked?**
....

Notes
....

Name
....

Services provided
....

Contact
....

Recommended by   **References checked?**
....

Notes
....

PROS TO CALL

Name
....

Services provided
....

Contact
....

Recommended by   **References checked?**
....

Notes
....

Name
....

Services provided
....

Contact
....

Recommended by   **References checked?**
....

Notes
....

Name
....

Services provided
....

Contact
....

Recommended by   **References checked?**
....

Notes
....

PROS TO CALL

Name

Services provided

Contact

Recommended by   **References checked?**

Notes

Name

Services provided

Contact

Recommended by   **References checked?**

Notes

I lost my to-do list, so I made a second to-do list, but then I found the first to-do list, which was slightly different than the second to-do list, so I made a new to-do list.

ITEMS LENT

Item	Borrower	Date	Notes	Returned?

ITEMS BORROWED

Item	Borrowed from	Date	Notes	Returned?

CODES & NOTES

Lock/security system location
....

Code
....

Notes/contacts
....

Lock/security system location
....

Code
....

Notes/contacts
....

Lock/security system location
....

Code
....

Notes/contacts
....

Lock/security system location
....

Code
....

Notes/contacts
....

Health at a Glance

Your health is important, but all the metrics and recommendations can be a lot to manage in your head. Control your blood pressure and swearing the next time you need to fill out yet *another* form by creating a picture of your health history and current care that you can turn to when you need it. Keep the information up-to-date, and let your loved ones know where they can find it.

TIPS

* Wrangle a list of prescriptions, supplements, and any over-the-counter meds you're taking here and also in your wallet or phone.
* Make yearly physicals easy to remember by scheduling them near your birthday or another special day. Plan a whole damn day dedicated to you!

THE BASICS

Allergies

....

Blood type	**Height**

....

Weight	**Date**

....

Weight	**Date**

....

Weight	**Date**

....

Weight	**Date**

....

Weight	**Date**

....

Weight	**Date**

....

I wandered around Target for an hour and called it a long walk.

MEDICATIONS & SUPPLEMENTS

Name	Dosage	Timing	Prescribed by	Reason

HEALTH CONDITIONS

Condition	Diagnosis	Date	Treatment

PAST SURGERIES & HOSPITALIZATIONS

Condition	Date	Notes

IMMUNIZATIONS

Date

Date

Date

Date

Date

Date

Date

Date

Date

Date

Date

Date

I hate it when I gain ten pounds for a role and then remember I'm not an actor.

PERSONAL HEALTH NOTES

....

....

....

....

....

....

....

....

....

....

....

....

....

....

....

My dentist told me I needed a crown.
I was like, "I know! Right?"

FAMILY HEALTH HISTORY

TESTS & SCREENINGS

Test	Date	Results	Next steps

TESTS & SCREENINGS

Test	Date	Results	Next steps

HEALTH GOALS

Goal
....

Action steps
....

....

....

Measures
....

....

....

Goal
....

Action steps
....

....

....

Measures
....

....

....

HEALTH GOALS

Goal
....

Action steps
....

....

....

Measures
....

....

....

Goal
....

Action steps
....

....

....

Measures
....

....

....

HEALTH CARE PROVIDERS

Name

Contact

Specialty

Visit dates

Name

Contact

Specialty

Visit dates

Name

Contact

Specialty

Visit dates

HEALTH CARE PROVIDERS

Name

Contact

Specialty

Visit dates

Name

Contact

Specialty

Visit dates

Name

Contact

Specialty

Visit dates

HEALTH INSURANCE

Provider   **Coverage**

....

ID number   **Group number**

....

Contact

....

Notes

....

Provider   **Coverage**

....

ID number   **Group number**

....

Contact

....

Notes

....

Provider   **Coverage**

....

ID number   **Group number**

....

Contact

....

Notes

....

On-the-Go Notes

Where was that little inn you stayed at and loved? "Near the water" probably isn't enough of a description to find it again. Where did you celebrate your last milestone birthday that made getting older not feel so bad? Record all those little shining stars where you spend time infrequently but want to come back to someday or recommend to someone else when the time is right.

TIPS

* If your magical place to remember doesn't have an address, use an online map to find GPS coordinates.
* To help keep your favorite places alive, post positive online reviews. Love a sketchy place you don't want to announce to the world? Use an alias for your reviews.

FAVORITE RESTAURANTS

Name   Location

Cuisine type   Pricing

Favorite menu item

Notes

Name   Location

Cuisine type   Pricing

Favorite menu item

Notes

Name   Location

Cuisine type   Pricing

Favorite menu item

Notes

FAVORITE RESTAURANTS

Name   **Location**

Cuisine type   **Pricing**

Favorite menu item

Notes

Name   **Location**

Cuisine type   **Pricing**

Favorite menu item

Notes

My memory is as useless as the "g" in lasagna.

BEST LODGING

Name   **Location**

Lodging type   **Pricing**

Notes

Name   **Location**

Lodging type   **Pricing**

Notes

Name   **Location**

Lodging type   **Pricing**

Notes

Name   **Location**

Lodging type   **Pricing**

Notes

BEST LODGING

Name   **Location**

Lodging type   **Pricing**

Notes

Name   **Location**

Lodging type   **Pricing**

Notes

Name   **Location**

Lodging type   **Pricing**

Notes

Name   **Location**

Lodging type   **Pricing**

Notes

FUN & ENTERTAINMENT

Name   **Location**
....

Venue type   **Pricing**
....

Notes
....

Name   **Location**
....

Venue type   **Pricing**
....

Notes
....

Name   **Location**
....

Venue type   **Pricing**
....

Notes
....

Name   **Location**
....

Venue type   **Pricing**
....

Notes
....

FUN & ENTERTAINMENT

Name   **Location**

Venue type   **Pricing**

Notes

Name   **Location**

Venue type   **Pricing**

Notes

Name   **Location**

Venue type   **Pricing**

Notes

Name   **Location**

Venue type   **Pricing**

Notes

EASY **TRAVEL**

Closest airports

....

....

Best airport parking

....

....

Taxi/car service

....

....

Passport number

....

Expiration date

....

The biggest lie I tell myself:
I don't need to write it down,
I'll remember it.

Where Did I Put That?

Stop stomping around as you try to locate your will or your passport, that special photo album or a treasured piece of jewelry! A simple written reminder may be all you need to get your act together. Preserve the locations of all those hidden treasures here.

TIPS

* Take your loved ones on a tour of the special items hidden in your home.
* Crap! Struggling to remember where you stashed something? Pretend you're hiding it for the first time. You just might come up with the original location.

HERE IT IS!

Treasure	Location

Some days, I amaze myself. Other days I put my phone in the freezer.